GWENNETH LEANE

Messages for the Minute

ILLUSTRATED BY
KYLIE LEANE

PUBLISHER
Kylie Margaret Leane
kmlpublishing.com

COVER ART/DESIGN/ILLUSTRATIONS
Kylie Leane

© 2022 Gwenneth Leane
All rights reserved.

No portion of this publication may be reproduced or transmitted,
in any form or by any means, without the prior written permission of either copyright owner or publisher of this book.

MESSAGES FOR THE MINUTE

Paperback Edition / March 2022 Gwenneth Leane
ISBN: 978-0-6451032-5-0

PRINTED IN AUSTRALIA

For information address:
gwen.leane@gmail.com
authorkylieleane@gmail.com

Gwenneth's Blog can be found online at:
www.wanderingwithwords.com

Messages for the Minute

CONTENTS

Courage	2
Faith	6
Fear	16
God	20
Heart	40
Hope	46
Jesus	66
Joy	78
Saved	84

Be as brave as a lion, whose roar creates terror.
Be as tenacious as a terrior.
Be strong in the LORD and keep your faith.
COURAGE says, don't be ashamed
that you love the LORD
Remember, the LORD great and awesome.
Continue in the LORD, know him more intimately.

Corinthians 16: 3

JESUS said:
Don't be afraid of anything, I will never leave you.
I am your strength you can overcome anything.
I am the beginning and end of your faith.
I am JESUS yesterday, today and forever.
I am SPIRIT says the LORD.
Worship me with your spirit.

John 4: 24

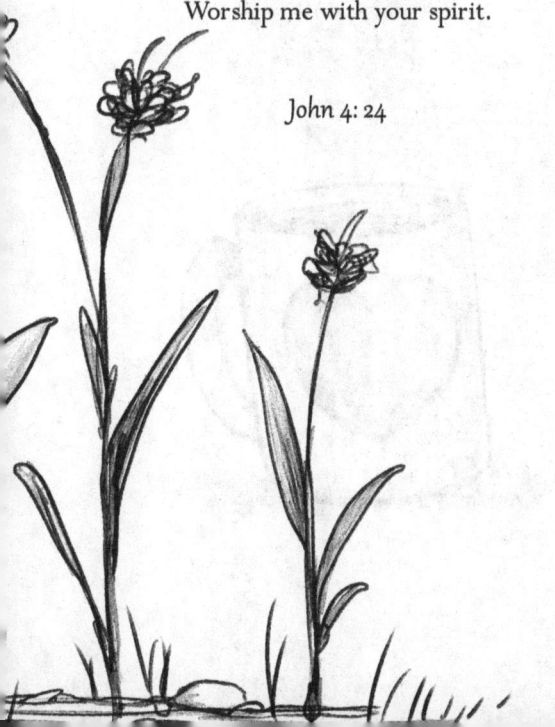

Faith says, seek the Lord
Faith says, you will find the Lord
Faith says, take God at his word
Faith says, all things are possible
Faith says, nothing is impossible
Faith says, believe and you will have what you believe.

Have faith in the living GOD, he will protect you.
Seek true knowledge of GOD
Do not allow yourself to be bewitched
by a lie dressed in truth.
Never be moved from the faith
JESUS said, *'See to it no one misleads you.'*

FAITH IS THE BEGINNING

Faith comes by believing in things unseen
Hope is the trust in what has not yet been.
Evil comes to those who evil think.
Lewd intentions bring a sensual wink.
Act slowly on raw emotions
Add to your heart your pure devotions
May love be your daily guide,
Even though from pain you hide.

A Christophersen ©

Faith that is stagnant leads
To not knowing JESUS
One cannot have an intimate
Relationship or walk with JESUS
And have a stagnant faith at the same time

2 Peter 3: 17-18

HIS VOICE

I give up my life because the voice of GOD calms me –
GOD's voice soothes – GOD's voice heals.
At his voice I grow, expand,
become the person I want to be.
His voice changes me and I am born again,
I become a news person –
Strong – everlasting.

FEAR NOT

Fear not flock of little number
It is you FATHER'S good pleasure
To give you the kingdom now
Trust in HIS Truth and Love.

From Luke 12;32
Arranged by A Christophersen

DO NOT FEAR

The LORD is my helper,
I will not fear.
Man can do nothing
That I need to fear.
GOD is my helper
In every time of need.
He is there always
And I trust in him now.

An adaption from Hebrews 13;6
A Christophersen

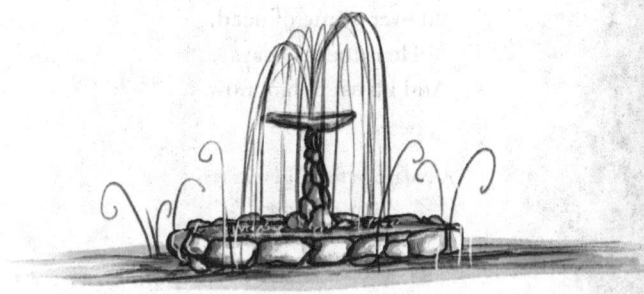

Truth is exact
Truth is pure
Truth slices through confusion
Truth dispels delusion.
Truth gives hope
Truth is wise
Truth does not make a mistake,
Truth forgives
Truth is JESUS
Take JESUS into the heart and be right with GOD.

John 14: 6

God satisfies the longing soul
God forgives the guilty heart.
God calms the terrified spirit
God strengthens the weary body.
God lifts the downhearted'
God gives courage to the weak.

Psalm 103

GOD doesn't lie
GOD has no favourites
GOD is not class conscious
GOD doesn't listen to tittle-tattle
GOD'S love is total, all inclusive
Enjoy GOD by accepting his SON, JESUS.

Definition of GOD
The only infinite eternal,
Unchangeable spirit
In whom all things begin
Continue and end.
JESUS CHRIST the sum of all things.

Hebrews 1: 2

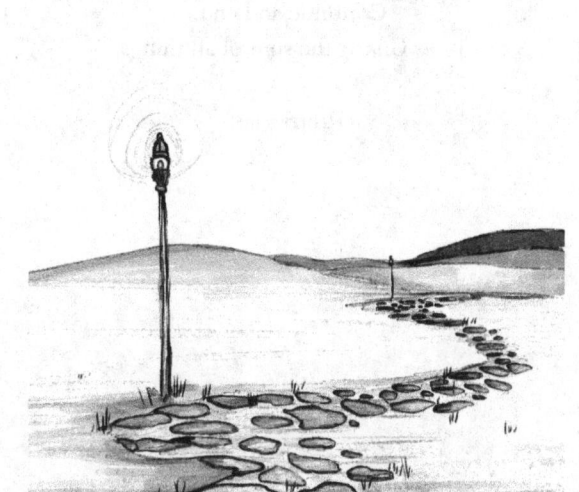

Your guidance has been as sure and
direct as day follows night.
By your hand
You have created a path
for all living creatures and
provides the sustenance to support them.
The seasons too, are unfailing in their cycle.
Yes! The cycles You have created bring
security and providence.
For Your providence, all creation,
And I give you praise.
You are the source of all my joy.

You are constant in Your care for
Your own but unpredictable
Because Your Mind
Is beyond even the imagination and intuition of man.
Your might is beyond imagination.
Because of the greatness of Your being
You are worthy of all praise.

You, O Lord, have chosen me not I you.
It is too immense for me to understand for even
before I was born you had a
plan and purpose for my life.
Even though I thought I was making the decisions,
I was unconsciously following the
path you had made for me.
How could I then not embrace
you with all of my heart.
Even when bad times come, I understand they are part
of your plan to make me grow.
The wonder of it all is that you do not leave me but
continue to reveal the path slowly
so that I can follow it.

You, LORD, light up my life.
Illuminate my mind increase my understanding,
making me aware of all creation.
You, LORD, are the CREATOR of light
because you are light.
Where you dwell there is not even a shadow.
To live with YOU is to live in light and with light.

The lion roars, the frog croaks and
the ibis stalks through the swamp.
You, LORD, provide for these
creatures daily, abundantly.
They praise you with their life.
They are the beautiful work of your hands.
They respond unconsciously to you in worship and
adoration for the life you have given them.
Only man makes an idol of creation.
Only man worships creation ignoring the CREATOR.
Only man endows creation with a power it does not
have and prays to it as though it were GOD.
Yet YOU continue to love man, elevating him to YOUR
throne room through JESUS your son.

The yoke of oppression is lifted by JESUS
The black hole of depression is filled by JESUS
Fear is dispelled by JESUS, the Prince of Peace
JESUS gives freedom and life.

Philippians 4: 6 – 7

Our heart, our soul is valuable real-estate.
We are owned by the power we serve.
God has paid a high ransom for us
God didn't use silver of gold
Jesus Christ is the ransom paid for our hearts.
Put away pride and independence
Change ownership
Live as a child of God

1 Corinthians 3: 16

The WORD is alive
The WORD Saves
The WORD frees from bondage
The WORD is eternal
The WORD is light
The WORD is knowledge
The WORD is wisdom
Hide the WORD in your heart

Psalm 119: 11

Wisdom is Compassion,
Wisdom is true judgement
Wisdom is understanding
Wisdom is empathetic
Wisdom is resolute
Wisdom is knowing God
Wisdom is unconditional love
Wisdom is gratefulness'
Wisdom is *Proverbs:1: 77*

Hope never gives up
Looks on the bright side,

But Now, Lord, what do I look for?
My hope is in you.

Psalm 39: 7

Hope never dies
Suggests another way:

May the GOD of hope fill you with
all peace as you trust in him
So that you may overflow with hope by the
power of the HOLY SPIRIT.

Romans 15: 13

Hope can be squashed
But springs up, born anew.

*'Blessed be the GOD and FATHER of our LORD JESUS CHRIST.
Because of his great mercy he has given us new berth
into a living hope through the resurrection of
JESUS CHRIST from the dead.'*
1 Peter 1: 3 CSB

Hope is always ready
To take another step.

*'So that your faith might not rest in the wisdom of men
but in the power of GOD.'
1 Corinthians 2: 5. ESV*

Hope is prepared
To take a knock.

*'For surely there is a future,
and your hope will not be cut off.'*
Proverbs 23:18

Hope is the stuff of success
If given full rein.

'For I know the plans I have for you,' declares the LORD,
'plans to prosper you and not harm you,
plans to give you hope and a future.'
Jeremiah 29:11

Hope stampedes
With enthusiasm.

*This hope is a strong and
trustworthy anchor for our souls.
It leads us through the curtain into
God's inner sanctuary.'
Hebrews 6: 19. NLT*

Hope doesn't stop
To count the cost.

*'Wherefore take unto you the whole armour of
God, that you may be able to withstand
in the evil day and having done all, to stand.'
Ephesians 6: 13*

Hope keeps on trying
Lasts forever.

'Three things will last forever — faith hope and love.'
1 Corinthians 13: 3. NLT

Hope is the backbone
Of life.

*'Let us hold tightly without wavering to the hope we affirm,
for GOD can be trusted to keep his promise.'
Hebrews 10: 23. NLT*

Jesus said:
I am the Son of God.
I am the Bread of life you will never hunger.
I am the Light of the world.
I am the way, the Truth and the Life
I am the Resurrection and the life.
I am with you forever.

John 10: 36

Jesus identified with us
Jesus tried in all points like us
Jesus rose from the grave
Jesus passed his resurrection life to us
Jesus gave us eternity
Accept Jesus as Saviour

Hebrews 4: 15

JESUS is the Way
JESUS is the Life
JESUS is the Truth
JESUS is the Light.
Life is Rich
When JESUS rules to the heart.

John 14: 6

I have decided to follow JESUS
Though no one follows me, I will still follow you
The cross is my beacon of light and life
I leave the world behind me
I will not turn back

Based on the song, 'I have decided to Follow JESUS'

Incarnation
GOD assumed Human nature
JESUS CHRIST the SON of GOD
JESUS is the actual form of GOD
JESUS is the human body of GOD
JESUS is the union of divinity
With human nature
JESUS the divine image of GOD

Hebrews 1: 3

I am anchored in you, not by my power but by JESUS.
Praise you for such profound truth
*'Or do you not realize about yourselves
that JESUS CHRIST is in you.'*

2 Corinthians 13: 5

Trust in the LORD with all your heart
Delight yourself in the LORD
Take pleasure in the LORD
Enjoy HIS presence
Delight to do HIS will
To obey is better than sacrifice.

Psalm 37:4

Being thankful clears the mind
Being thankful dispels anxiety
Being thankful calms fear
Being thankful brings happiness
Being thankful brings answered prayer
Being thankful gives courage to go forward.

Philippians 4: 6-7

Jesus is Joy
Jesus shares his joy with us
We never lose his joy
His joy may tarnish
Because the devil lied to us
We never lost his joy
Because once Jesus gives
He never takes away again.

John 15: 11

I choose to love GOD with all of my being.
I choose to serve GOD wholeheartedly.
I choose to belong to GOD and remain with him.
I choose to be dependent on GOD alone.
I choose eternal life through JESUS CHRIST.
I choose intimacy with GOD and
share in his life and blesssings.

Psalm 25:12-14

Choose righteousness and wisdom
Choose nobility and purity of thought
Choose to give generously
Choose to give praise and not criticism
Choose to live by the HOLY SPIRIT and not by feelings
Choose today to depend on GOD alone.

Philippians 4: 8

I am saved by Jesus.
I believe Jesus died for me
I am forgiven of the past, the present, the future,
wrong doing
I am a new person in Christ
I no longer live but Christ in me
I have eternal life through Christ Jesus.

'For it is by grace that you have been saved through faith, and this not of yourselves: it is the gift of God.'
Ephesians 2: 8

Eternity,
A state which has no application,
It is timeless
It is endless life, after death
Eternity is immeasurable,
Infinity.
Time begins in eternity
Stretching to eternity
Jesus is eternity.

1 John 1: 1 - 2

ABOUT THE AUTHOR

GWENNETH LEANE

My writing life is like a rainbow cake – layer upon layer.
The first layer was compiling the church news-letter. It was illustrated, and newsy.
No church news-letter was ever like it.

Then came the journalistic layer. Great heights were reached with an article in the Women's Weekly and working as a journalist for the local newspaper, The Transcontinental. There were farming and gardening magazines included in that layer.
The biography layer came next. Three biographies were self-published. Several other short biographies written. It is so interesting and necessary to record people's stories for history's sake.

Like cream between the layers I practised the art of short story writing.
The present layer is blogging. I have a blog site and it covers my writing life from short stories, journalistic articles, photography, and anything that demands to be written and read.
I love this writing life.

Learn more about Gwenneth's Writings at:
www.wanderingwithwords.com

ABOUT THE ILLUSTRATOR

KYLIE LEANE

Kylie Leane is the author of *The Dynasty of Earth and Stars* and its expanded universe.

She lives in a little cottage, with her pet cats, Winter and Charcoal. Between writing, drawing - and now university - she enjoys spending time in her garden, going for long walks, watching anime, playing a good video game, and curling up by the fire in winter.

She hopes to someday expand KML Publishing – for bringing stories to life and making beautiful books is one of her greatest passions in life.

Being dyslexic does cause some trouble, and self-publishing is one mountain after another, but the reward of telling stories is worth all the hassle.

kmlpublishing.com

www.ingramcontent.com/pod-product-compliance
Lightning Source LLC
Chambersburg PA
CBHW011148290426
44109CB00023B/2529